KEY TO DEEP CHANGE STUDY

SMALL GROUP GUIDE

Second Edition

Further training based on the book
The Key to Deep Change:
Experiencing Spiritual Transformation
by Facing Unfinished Business

DR. STEVE AND SHIRLEY SMITH

This small group experience is based on the book,

The Key to Deep Change: Experiencing Spiritual Transformation by Facing Unfinished Business

by Dr. Steve Smith.

Available from ChurchEquippers.com

TABLE OF CONTENTS

WELCOME TO THE KEY TO DEEP CHANGE SMALL GROUP EXPERIENCE.

This experience is for people who have read *The Key to Deep Change: Experiencing Spiritual Transformation by Facing Unfinished Business* by Dr. Steve Smith (available from ChurchEquippers.com), or have gone through the *Unfinished Business Seminar* or have participated in an *Upgrade: Preparing the Soil Retreat*. This experience will be less helpful if you do not have a basic understanding of transformation from those resources. You can find out more about these resources at

www.ChurchEquippers.com

There will be 10 weekly sessions of 1½ hours each. To be a participant, you must already be a Christian and part of a church family. Without the presence of the Spirit in your life, you will not be able to grasp and utilize the experience's concepts.

Also, for this experience to be most effective for you, you should be part of a group of 8 or less that is either men or women only. Many of the lessons ask for personal information that would be difficult to share in front of those of the opposite sex and probably even before your spouse. Therefore, you need to be a man with men or a woman with women. Otherwise the experience will be much less effective and the level of interaction will be pretty shallow at best. The added benefit of this is that those in your group will become your lifelong faith community, people who will stand with you to encourage and restore you even as you do the same for them as you journey together with God.

Every group will be led by an experienced facilitator who is already on his or her own faith journey towards transformation. Remember that this person has not yet finished the journey and may share his or her own unfinished business during the experience. Do not be shocked and do not allow yourself to think that you cannot learn anything from someone who is not perfect, because there is just no one who is perfect yet except Jesus. And he will be present in the room with you as this experience goes on.

The following book is full of the questions that will be asked. They will help you, the participant, to be prepared to address whatever aspect of your unfinished business God is revealing to you through this experience. Make sure to write out answers to the questions and interactions for yourself so you will be ready to share with the other participants. Make sure to bring a Bible so you can look up the Scriptures during your time together, so you can see for yourself what God has said, and that what He has said has authority and meaning for your life.

It is important also that you do the homework. You will not grow through these sessions if you neglect this part of the process. Each homework assignment is to prepare you for the next session. So to not prepare says something about your desire to grow and be transformed.

May you hear God speaking to you during this experience. He loves you unconditionally and has already determined to conform you into the likeness of Jesus. Listen to Him carefully.

Peace!

SESSION 1: THE POWER TO CHANGE HAS BEEN GIVEN

Introduction: The Facilitator's Testimony—personal story of God's transformational power in facilitator's life.

1. Why are you here? Some of you are here because it is the right thing to do, but are also questioning whether or not you need this interaction. You may feel that you are managing your life with God and others very well.

2. All people who follow Jesus get stuck someplace at some time in their faith journey. The reason for this is because we still are affected by what the Bible calls the "flesh." Look up the following verses for an understanding of what is meant by flesh: 1 John 2:15-17; Galatians 5:19-21; Ephesians 2:1-3.

   Although we may naturally equate the flesh life to being openly wicked, flesh takes different forms in people's lives. Sometimes the flesh life looks pretty respectable. Look at the five kinds of flesh demonstrated by different people who encountered Jesus.

   A. **Prime:** religiously successful (John 3:1, 10: Nicodemus)

   B. **Choice:** materially successful (Luke 19:1-4: Zacchaeus)

   C. **Standard:** store brand variety that could be either a good or bad choice (Luke 5:8-10; Matthew 16: 15-16, 22-23: Peter)

   D. **Utility:** living life all ground up by immaturity, bad choices and limited prospects (John 4:1-20: Woman at the well)

   E. **Waste:** marked as useless and tossed out (John 8:1-5: Woman caught in adultery)

   - With which flesh life would you be most closely identified? Why?

3. Read the following statement and verses and answer this question: Why is the flesh life so destructive for those who follow it?

The flesh life means that we are following the desires that come from within us to try to get our personal needs met and to make us feel better and in control apart from God.

4. Which of the following are true for you?

    - I continually talk or think about the same subject and know I am stuck.

    - I am or have been made aware of unhealthy character issues that do not match the character of Jesus as revealed in the Bible.

    - I constantly go to extremes in some area of my life.

    - I am experiencing tensions in my marriage.

    - I have been in continual financial trouble.

    - I often feel afraid in some way.

    - I feel exhausted and burnt out.

    - I am going through a personal crisis.

    - Other people have made me aware that I make derogatory or demeaning statements about myself or others.

    - Other people have made me aware that I make outrageous or irrational statements

5. Review of the Heart Chart

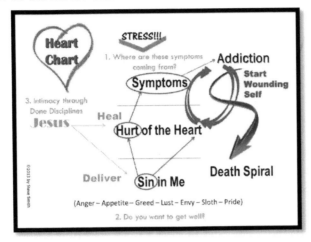

You can find an overview of this chart at:
www.churchequippers.com/heart-chart/

6. What do you understand about the relationship between being wounded and making choices?

7. What did you learn about yourself from this chart so far?

8. Read this statement and answer the following question: In what ways have you been camouflaging the damaged parts of your life?

Right now, you may have a bunch of issues overwhelming you. You may feel defeated by the way you live. You may be using camouflage to keep people from seeing these parts of your life. (Religion is one example, but another is being socially outgoing or its opposite—being very private. Or being indispensable and handy so no one will ask questions. Or controlling people and information. Or putting on a happy face. Smokescreens come in numerous forms.) But you know the hidden issues slip out. And if no one else knows, your family does. Moreover, you have a backstage view of yourself. You know the truth.

9. Who here are still wondering if and where you are stuck spiritually on your faith journey? Look up Psalm 139:23-24 and answer the

following question: If I want to be on a journey to wholeness and maturity, am I willing to ask God to do a ruthless search of my soul to discover what He wants to transform in me?

10. How do you understand Romans 8:29 as the practical application of the gospel in your life? If you were to be conformed to the likeness of Jesus, how would you be different on the inside and on the outside from what you are right now?

11. In terms of our opportunity to live a new life, the difference between those who live a reformed life and a transformed life is simply their source of strength to live the life.

REFORMATION = God's truth lived out in my strength
TRANSFORMATION = God's truth lived out in His strength—which is the biblical idea of "grace"

As a group, discuss what the difference would be in living out your life as a believer by transformation instead of reformation.

12. Do you have a hard time with believing God wants to change you personally? If so, why? If not, why are you stuck in the process?

13. Read and discuss the following statement. How is this truth different from what you have heard before?

"My grace is sufficient for you for my power is made perfect in weakness" (2 Corinthians 12:9-10). What Paul says is that God wants to show His strength when we are ready to acknowledge our weakness. Here's the point: Maturity is discovering how weak I am. In all of these areas where I feel that I'm failing, where I'm depending on the flesh to get my needs met, God isn't calling me to get stronger so I won't make those wrong decisions anymore. He's calling me into an intimate relationship where I'm dependent on him to do all of this for me. That's the good news. It's not about trying harder or just changing my mind. I'm going to get well by believing God and trusting His power to take care of these things for me.

How am I going to stop my symptoms? By gritting my teeth and trying hard to quit them? By focusing my attention on the problem? NO. I'm going to stop doing them by admitting that I cannot stop doing them, and by focusing on Jesus and depending on His power to change me from the inside and stop these things for me. Ask yourself, "What are my expectations from this course? Why am I here? Do I want anything to come out of this? Do I really expect to change?"

14. Discuss the implications of this illustration.

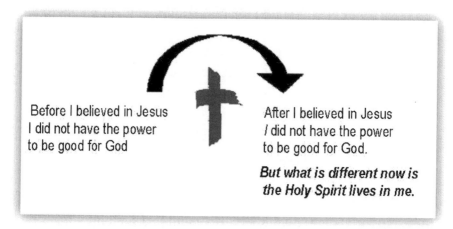

Before I believed in Jesus I did not have the power to be good for God

After I believed in Jesus I did not have the power to be good for God.

But what is different now is the Holy Spirit lives in me.

Does it make you feel hopeful or discouraged?

At the end of this session: Pair up and pray with another person. Share something from your personal journey that you need prayer about. Then pray for the other person's need.

Homework Assignment: Next week we will be studying the way we got into our mess. To prepare for this lesson, please make a private list of everyone you have a broken or strained relationship with, including God. Ask God why each relationship was strained or broken.

Read Romans 5:9/10. Spend 15 minutes this week thinking about how you came to trust Jesus for your salvation. What changes have come into your life that matter to you? How much more do you want God to change you?

SESSION 2: WHY WE STRUGGLE IN OUR MESS

1. Review homework. What does your list of broken or strained relationships tell you about where you are?

2. If you are willing, share one of your strained/broken relationships. In what ways have you been blaming the other person for the break in this relationship? Where are you in owning your part in the strained or broken relationship?

3. Read the Garden story of Genesis 3:1-19. In what ways are your strained/broken relationships related to the Garden story?

4. Read the following passage and answer these questions: How much of your life is bound up in secret keeping?

Whereas before they had no barriers between them, forever after they felt the need to cover up and hide. Shame became the watchword of all relationships. I don't know about you, but of all the friends I have had, I never, not even in my deepest relationships, have experienced a time when one of us wasn't hiding something from the other, when we could not quite reveal all that we wanted to. Why is this issue so important? Because we were created by a unique being whose essence is love. What the Fall did to us was to rob us of our ability to receive love from Him and to give it to each other.

It is a basic human desire to be known without reservation by another. And not just to be known, but to be loved unconditionally by that person no matter what is true about us. Much of our lives turns on this desire. We are out looking for love, whether or not we are conscious of this search. Or despairing of it, for we may have already found that most love is conditional. We think people will love us if we keep hidden the full truth about ourselves. We think we cannot be transparent because that will mean rejection. Or we think the truth about ourselves can be dangerous because it might give someone else power over us. Some of us learned this the hard way. Some know it instinctively.

- Why do you believe this is or is not so?
- Have you blamed the other person for what is wrong in your life?
- Read Proverbs 4:18-19 and Mark 4:22 and apply them to this question: What is God's plan for those who belong to Him concerning secret-keeping and secret-telling?

5. Are there areas in your life where doing what you prefer, such as defiance, unforgiveness, going your own way, etc., brought more damage to your strained/broken relationships?

6. Do you believe that these strained/broken relationships will go on for the rest of your life? If no, what will need to heal in you to change the strained/broken relationships that you currently have?

7. Why do you think that we act the way we do?

8. Overview of the impact of the Fall in Genesis 3. According to 1 Thessalonians 5:23, humans have three aspects to their being— body, soul and spirit. We have a body formed from the dust of the earth into which God breathed spirit so that we became living souls (Genesis 2:7). Each aspect relates to a different realm of the creation, as seen in the following chart. Discuss the implications of the Fall on how a person without God will live out his or her life.

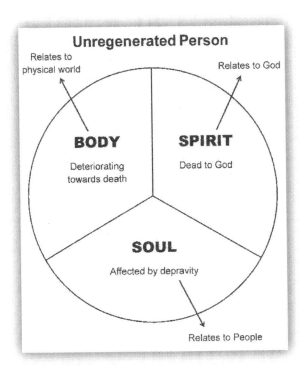

9. Look at the chart on the next page. Answer the following questions about it:

- Where are you as a child of God in the process of salvation?
- What does it reveal about why people like you who know God continue to struggle with making damaging choices and ignoring the work of the Spirit in your life?

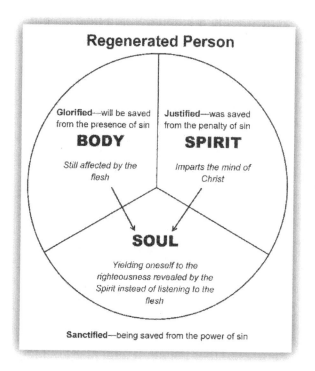

Regenerated Person

Glorified—will be saved from the presence of sin
BODY

Still affected by the flesh

Justified—was saved from the penalty of sin
SPIRIT

Imparts the mind of Christ

SOUL

Yielding oneself to the righteousness revealed by the Spirit instead of listening to the flesh

Sanctified—being saved from the power of sin

10. Read Romans 6:3-9. The resurrection reversed the impact of the Fall on us, restoring us from death back to what God created us to be.

- What will you be like when this process is completed in you?
- How will you be different? The same?
- How do you see this affecting how you live your life and your relationships?

11. If asked by God, what would be the last thing you honestly would not want to give up in your life, be it a relationship, a prized possession, a pursuit, a way of thinking, a position, etc.?

- Why would giving this up be difficult?
- How does this stack up with God's reign over you?

12. Read the following truth and answer this question: What causes you to struggle emotionally, if not rationally, with the claim that God loves you?

Here is truth about love. As a human, your deepest desire is to be loved. This is why you are exploring this journey. What you are looking for in life is God. Not just because God is loving but because God is Love. His being defines love, so all His actions towards you are rooted in love. Your needs are driving you towards God, not away from God. The dividing issue between you and God is not the consequences of your choices but: Who is going to be in charge of getting your needs met?

13. Read Romans 12:1-2. The lies that you may believe about yourself and others reveal that Satan has gotten to you through your mind. You may be repeating these lies to yourself on a daily basis. Renewing of your mind involves the lies of the enemy being rooted out by the truth of who God is and your relationship to Him. You cooperate with the Holy Spirit in this process by:

- Recognizing and naming the lie.
- Replacing it with God's truth, even when your emotions are rejecting this. Truth comes when the Spirit makes the revelation about God clear to you.
- Living the truth by the power of the Holy Spirit.

Discuss how this process could change how you see yourself and the people with whom you are in strained/broken relationship.

At the end of this session: Pair up and pray with another person. Share something from your personal journey that you need prayer about. Then pray for the other person's need.

Homework Assignment: Next week we will be studying our true identity as sons and daughters of God. In preparation for this, please read through Colossians 1-3, looking for every place it says you are "in Christ" or "with Christ." These two phrases are Paul's shorthand way of talking about our true identity. As you spot each one, write out the truth you discover by using the following statement:

In Christ I am/have _____.

Examples:

1:5   I have hope stored up for me in Heaven in Christ Jesus.
1:11   I am strengthened with all power according to His glorious might in Christ Jesus.

Read Psalm 46. Spend 15 minutes this week processing what you think about God when you think about God, especially in the confusing and painful moments of your life. How has your faith in Him changed?

SESSION 3: IDENTITY IN CHRIST – WHO AM I?

1. Read the following statement and answer these questions: Why are people afraid to reveal what they struggle with inside? How does this kind of secrecy affect their journey to wholeness?

Proverbs 27:19 says, "As a face is reflected in water, so the heart reflects the person." There is stuff going on inside of you, some of which you won't even admit to yourself—let alone anyone else—and it does not match in any way what you are portraying to people on the outside.

2. Circle of transformation illustrates the journey to wholeness.

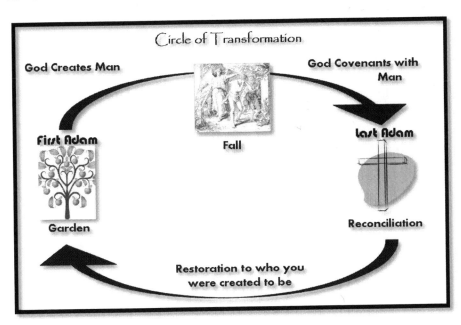

- What characterized the First Adam in his being and relationship with God according to Genesis 2:7-25?

- Read Romans 5:12, 15-19. What was the impact on human beings of the choices of the First Adam? How has the Second Adam changed the life situation for those who believe?

- How is Jesus as the Second Adam related to what Paul says in Romans 8:29?

3. Review Homework. The story of the Garden reveals to us that we are the descendants of Adam. The story of the gospel tells us we are now children of God. Paul uses the phrase "in Christ" many times in his writing to express this truth. So who are you "in Christ"?

4. Read through Ephesians 1-3 together. What do you find about yourself in these verses that is true from being "in Christ"? As you read this together, again complete the following statement: "In Christ I am/have_____." When finished, discuss how this relates to God conforming you to the likeness of Jesus.

5. Whatever you see broken and sinful inside you is not who you really are, although it may be what you are experiencing at the moment. Read the following statement and discuss its implications for your personal journey.

When God comes into my heart the old me goes and all that is left is the new me. 2 Corinthians 5:17 "If any man is in Christ he is a new creation." What is a creation? That means something has been formed that didn't exist previously. Something is made out of nothing. God did this in me and in you. In another lesson we talked about the three aspects of humans (body, soul, and spirit). The Hebrew view of humanity is not that we have three parts—there is no such thing as a soul existing separate from a body. We are soul, we are spirit, and we are body. And if any of these elements are gone, that person no longer exists in this reality. There are no loose souls floating around in our world. When we were dead in our sins (upon being born into this world), we were dead in the aspect of spirit—not in our soul (our personality, mind, will) or our body. When Jesus came into us by way of the Holy Spirit we were given a living spirit to replace this dead one. So to say we have an old me inside of us which fights against the new me is to totally misunderstand the scripture. There is no old me. There is a new me. My new identity is as a CHILD OF GOD. John 1:12 "To all who received him, to those who believed in his name, he gave the right to become children of God." Romans 8:14-15 "Those who are led by the Spirit of God are sons of God. We have not received a spirit of fear but a spirit of sonship by which we cry "Abba (or daddy) to God." Galatians 3:26 – 4:7 talks of us being "his children and an heir." I John 3:1,2 "When we see Jesus we will be like him." That's our identity. We are no longer sinners. We were sinners. I was a sinner. But now I am a child of God. That is my identity. That is my identity for life.

6. Read Romans 6:1-6 and apply it to the following picture. What do these verses say about how this change in your identity was accomplished? What does it mean to be baptized into Christ's death?

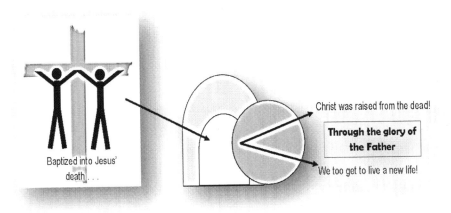

Baptized into Jesus' death . . .

Christ was raised from the dead!

Through the glory of the Father

We too get to live a new life!

7. Why do we continually forget how important this truth is for us? Read Romans 6:19. Relate this verse to Genesis 3:4 and John 8:44.

8. Do you still have a hard time believing that God wants to change you personally?

At the end of this session: Pair up and pray with another person. Share something from your personal journey that you need prayer about. Then pray for the other person's need.

Homework Assignment: Next week we are looking at symptoms, which are outward and observable behaviors and attitudes that cause people pain and/or are barriers between them and others. Using the Symptom Discovery Inventory, develop as comprehensive a list of your personal symptoms as you are able. A downloadable inventory worksheet is available to help with this process at:

www.ChurchEquippers.com/downloadables/

Read Psalm 23. Spend 15 minutes meditating on what is means for you to have God as your shepherd.

SESSION 4: IDENTIFYING YOUR STUFF

1. Review symptom inventory homework. What are some of the symptoms in your life that you are willing to share with the group?

2. How do people become addicted? What does addiction mean for someone who is not abusing drugs or alcohol?

3. Of your personal symptoms, which ones would you say have passed into being addictions?

4. What parts of your life are being affected by your addictions?

5. How do these addictions form your personal identity? (Do you or others have a descriptive name for you?)

6. Review the four failed strategies that people turn to in order to deal with their symptoms.

Repression*: Trying to get healthy by keeping the problem out of sight, a strategy of self-deception. We decide we will not look at it anymore, that we will defeat it by ignoring it altogether.*

Lateral Moves*: This tactic of change comes in many different forms, but it always amounts to the same thing—making external changes without inner transformation.*

Blame Game*: No matter who, the cause of your unfinished business is someone's fault and you want them to take the responsibility to fix it if it is going to be addressed at all.*

Outward Conformity*: Perhaps the most misunderstood tactic to which people resort looks the most Christian. "Just be obedient. Follow what* *the Bible says and you will be changed. Submit your unfinished business to God and obey."*

- Which is the one you see yourself using most often to fix or protect yourself and why?

7. Discuss the difference between reformation (God's truth done in my strength) and transformation (God's truth done through the empowering Holy Spirit).

- How does the distinction between these two explain the failed strategies you have been using to fix or protect yourself up to now?

8. Look up Romans 8:29. Compare your personal identity with that of the character of Jesus. How do you understand God at work in your addictions to conform you to Jesus' likeness?

9. Symptoms always indicate deeper issues inside us. Talk about where you think these symptoms/addictions are coming from.

- How does talking about this subject affect you emotionally?
- What do you need to learn from the Holy Spirit on this?

10. Look up John 5:1-16.

- What was the key question that Jesus asked?
- Why was that question important?
- What if he had said "no"?
- What did the man's response in verse 7 reveal about the man's attempts to get well?
- Why do you think Jesus made him take up his mat on a Sabbath day?
- How do you understand the question Jesus is asking in terms of your own need to get well?

- Where are you personally at in responding to Jesus' question? Which words capture where you are at this moment? Hope. Trust. Fear. Questions. Determination. Anger. Surrender.

11. Read the following quote and answer these questions: Do you personally have a hard time believing this about God?

How does God respond to you at this point? Is God disgusted with you? Have you been brought up to believe that other people are more loved and accepted by God because they appear to have it all together? Look at **Hosea 11:1-4** *God is saying, "Look what I have done to bring my people out of slavery."* **11:8-9** *"I am God and not man." God does not respond to us like we think He should or might. He loves us unconditionally, so that even in our mess, He still loves us and plans to restore us. We deserve judgment but God doesn't respond to us in that way. He isn't like people. He doesn't say, "Well you can be with my church people but you have to sit on the back row and keep your mouth shut because you're damaged goods."*

- How safe do you feel about God's love for you?
- What would it take for you to be ready to ask God to do a ruthless search of your heart to show you what you need to know to get well?

At the end of this session: Pair up and pray with another person. Share something from your personal journey that you need prayer about. Then pray for the other person's need.

Homework Assignment: Next week we will be focused on how and why people are wounded. Schedule time before God this week and do the *Hurt of the Heart Inventory* which can be found at:

www.ChurchEquippers.com/downloadables/

Read Colossians 3:1-3. Spend 15 minutes thinking how your earthly life in the past contrasts to the life Jesus is giving you now. Are you where you want to be on your faith journey?

SESSION 5: HURT OF THE HEART

1. Read Matthew 12:34 and 15:18-19. In the Bible the heart is a place where emotions and rational thoughts are weighed out to make decisions about life. Discuss how this definition affects your view of your own life decisions.

2. Discuss the implications of the following picture in light of your own life. Describe a decision you have made that you now know was made by your damaged emotions overriding your rational thinking.

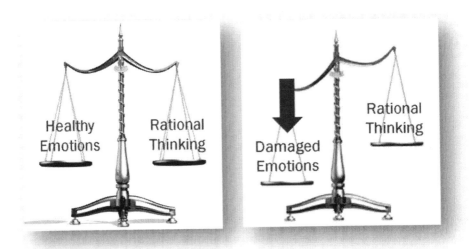

3. Review homework. What did you discover about your emotional history?

4. Discuss the idea of layers of wounds. Sometimes the wounds remembered are the most recently inflicted. It is helpful to connect symptoms or addictions in your life with the time you were first

wounded. Do you see a cycle of similar painful events in your life story? How far back can you remember the appearance of your symptoms?

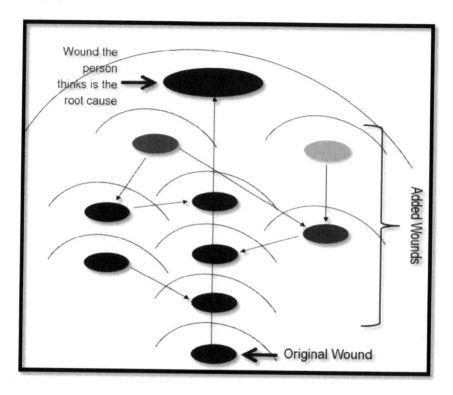

5. Read the following story and answer the following questions: What kind of wounds do you think this woman had? What choices did she make to deal with her wounds? Why do you think she made those choices?

Frank reached out to help a woman caught in a staggering situation. Raised by a secure family of Jesus followers, she married a promising young businessman. Together they experienced financial success and brought some great kids into the world. Then things went awry. The husband's improper business decisions led to a long prison term. His assets were grabbed to pay back creditors. She was suddenly left with no money to live on and no job skills to market. All of these events—her husband's imprisonment coupled with the loss of their life together, plus the painful embarrassment of their situation and facing the future alone and untrained—were major wounds. Frank hired her into his company and helped her to earn the kind of income she needed to live. Except, to the horrified astonishment of all who watched, she began to pursue a sexual relationship with a married man who worked there. Frank took her aside and counseled her time after time about the damage she was doing to herself and her children and how she was betraying Jesus. Nothing he said was heard. She mistressed this man until he finally divorced his wife. She divorced her jailed husband and they married. The rest of the story was full of sadness also. Why did she do this? Nothing in her background even hinted she would live out a sordid story like this. She had never stepped outside the boundaries of decency, had been a loving daughter, wife, and mother. She never stopped going to church, even during her pursuit of this man.

6. Reflect further on the previous story by reading the following statement. Then answer these questions: In what ways are damaged emotions a real danger to you? Who is behind the lies your damaged emotions relay to you? Why is it important to know this?

We'd say that most people in this room are fairly normal. But there are certain things that I might say to you that would set your damaged emotions off. In most areas you're fine, but in certain areas your emotions still rule, still tell you what reality is. You can sit down with some people and they seem to be so normal until you start talking to them about their marriage or some other topic. Then they suddenly get hot, they get emotional, and tears come to their eyes or they stick out their jaw and grit their teeth. And you say, "Ooh what's going on here, why are they acting that way?" Well, in that area of their life they got hurt, and the hurt of their heart has affected their emotions so much that they can't talk rationally about that area. Their emotions have created a false reality. And if you dare to contradict what they are saying about this issue in any way and say that really isn't true, their anger would be turned toward you. Why? Because their emotions say "this is reality and if you don't accept reality you are lying to me. Who is lying to them? You are not lying to them. Their emotions are lying to them. Sin in their heart is using their emotions to tell them lies that are directing their lives. And people make decisions based on these things. And these decisions lead them somewhere. It can lead them to destruction. Do you think that the hurts of your heart that you remember were inflicted deliberately, accidentally, or thoughtlessly?

- Why do you think the person(s) who inflicted the wounds did that to you?
- Were you made to "feel" that the wounding was your fault?
- How has that person(s) actions affected your ability to receive love from him or her?

7. People most often try to deal with wounds internally. In the process, they develop self-talk (Examples: You did it again...Give it up...You are so stupid...I am better than that idiot...I have to use/look/eat...I feel so alone...No one cares about me).

- What is the nature of your self-talk and what does it reveal about your current self-understanding?
- Which of the following have appeared in your life because of being wounded: 1) Denial that what happened affected you; 2) A sense of loss and victimhood; 3) A belief that you are powerless to do anything to get over it; 4) a determination to prove yourself.

8. Were you a Christian at the time when you received the wounds you remember? If you were, how did the wounds affect your relationship with God?

9. Read the following statement and answer this question: What do you understand has to happen between you and God in order for you to move towards healing?

This is about being honest about my wounds. I want to go away admitting that, "yes, I have wounds that I have not let God deal with."

At the end of this session: Pair up and pray with another person. Share something from your personal journey that you need prayer about. Then pray for the other person's need.

Homework Assignment: Next week we will be working through sin choices that damage us. Please schedule time to do the Deadly Sin Inventory. It is quite lengthy and will take extra time. You will find it online at:

www.ChurchEquippers.com/downloadables/

Read Romans 8:15.Spend 15 minutes thinking about areas of your life where you still experience fear. How does being a child of God offer you freedom from those fears?

SESSION 6: SIN IN ME

1. What have you learned about yourself so far? How has this new self-understanding affected you emotionally? Spiritually?

2. Read the following statement and answer this question: What is the difference between comfort and healing?

We were not created by God to be able to handle pain in our souls. Because we cannot live with pain, we are looking for relief from the pain. That brings us all to the crossroads of choice. What we choose will take us towards gaining health or increasing the damage. While this is not a once-for-all-time choice, never to be revisited, regretted and revoked, choices are sending our lives towards one or the other destination every moment we live. It doesn't matter how spiritual you believe you are or how good an upbringing you had. Pain demands comfort and our background will not prevent us from choosing something for comfort which leads a destructive destination.

3. Read Romans 7:14-23.

   • What is Paul revealing about his own journey towards being conformed to the likeness of Jesus?

   • What is the difference between sins that we do and *sin in me*?

   • Why do you think we prefer to choose sin over being made whole?

4. Discuss the Seven Deadly Sins and the symptoms. Connect the related symptoms of the seven sins to your personal family history.

Pride: *"I am the center of my world, so I will do what I prefer."*
Related symptoms: drive for power and control, dissension, isolation, defensiveness, selfish ambition, bragging, overly aggressive, overly competitive, factions, witchcraft, legalism, lying, superiority, ostentation, self-affirmation

Appetite (Gluttony): *"I have to indulge."* Related symptoms: appetites, drugs, sexual attachments, alcohol, overeating, spending, collecting, workaholism, attachment to relationships, high-stake risk taking

Lust: *"I desire sexual pleasure without boundaries."* Related symptoms: immorality, impurity, debauchery, pornography, homosexuality, serial relationships, incest, bestiality, married but on the hunt, inappropriate touching, course joking, orgies, sexual staring

Anger: *"I am offended and will get even."* Related symptoms: hatred, discord, rage, slander, violence, brawling, argumentative, bitterness, rebellion, rape, divorce, holding grudges

Greed: *"I want more and more."* Related symptoms: accumulation, income dissatisfaction, hoarding, refusing to be generous, idolatry, gambling, ignoring the poor

Envy: *"I deserve what they have."* Related symptoms: alienation, disappointment, strife, division, gossip, jealousy, undermining others, finger pointing, inferiority

Sloth: *"I am not responsible for myself."* Related symptoms: depression, non-change decisions, poor self-image, panic attacks, self-sabotage, victimhood, laziness, blame-shifting, lack of educational interest

5. Review homework.

   - How did your beginning estimation compare with the actual inventory?
   - Were you surprised by the result? Why?
   - How do you personally feel about what you discovered through this inventory?

6. All sin is addictive. When you see yourself acting in certain ways, you know you have made an internal decision to comfort yourself

apart from God. Read the following statement and answer this question: Why do you have to accept both of these as true?

There are two truths you have to acknowledge about addiction if you are going to find freedom. The first is that addiction is powerful—much more powerful than you are. This is not just about drugs or alcohol. All addictions are powerful. You will not be able to stop on your own, no matter how hard you try. Whatever you are addicted to has allied itself with your damaged emotions. Through them, it is ruling over your will even when your rational thoughts warn you of its destructive work. Your mind can see where the addiction is leading you, but your so-called "free will" will not respond with a rescue, even if you are on the brink of death. That's how powerful addiction is.

The second truth is that you really enjoy what you are addicted to. They are pleasure activities. It's no use Christianizing our dilemma. We look at pornography because we like the feeling we get when seeing naked people. We get even with those who hurt us and love it. We revel in overeating—you cannot have too much pie! Our road rage is justified and do we ever feel righteous. There is always tomorrow to find a job, so we enjoy our TV marathon today with no guilt. And who doesn't love spending money, even if we will have to rob Peter to pay Paul? Whatever our addiction, we do it again and again because it makes us feel good at some level, even though it is leading us to destruction. We lie to others, even ourselves, on this point because we know we are supposed to hate sin. But it is such fun! It is this aspect of addiction that draws us in even as we desperately ask Jesus to rescue us.

7. Review the two things we need Jesus to do for us. Which is the harder one for you to ask Him for?

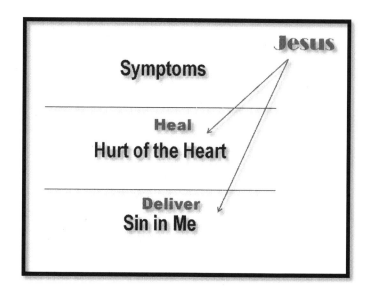

8. Count the cost on this question. What do you really want to do about your inside issues? Do you really want to get well?

9. Read James 5:16. Why do you think confession leads to healing?

   • What are the *sin in me* choices which you are aware you have made that you need Jesus to deliver you from? Are you ready to confess and repent of these choices?
   • Do you understand what "repentance" means?

10. Study Galatians 5:22-25. This passage is about the Great Exchange—what God gives us in place of the deadly sins.

    • How does the fruit of the Spirit counteract the deadly sins in your life?
    • What does Paul mean by "let us keep in step with the Spirit"?
    • How does keeping in step with the Spirit bring change and wholeness to your life?

At the end of this session: Pair up and pray with another person. Share something from your personal journey that you need prayer about. Then pray for the other person's need.

Homework Assignment: This is a different kind of assignment. This week, when you spend time alone with God, you are to take a full 60 seconds and be quiet before the Father. This is not a prayer time, but a listening/receiving time from God. Start by reading Hebrews 4:14-16. As you are ready, recognize you are in God's presence. Tell Him you are ready to receive from Him whatever He has for you. Be quiet and listen for His voice. After the time is finished, write out what you experienced in that time. If possible, practice being in His presence in this way every day this week.

Read Romans 8:31-39. Spend 15 minutes meditating about when you first began to know that God's love for you was different from the love other people in your life had for you. What memory does this bring to your mind?

SESSION 7: INTIMACY THROUGH REST

1. What have you learned about yourself so far? How has this new self-understanding affected you emotionally? Spiritually?

2. Read the following statement and answer the following question: Why would *to stop trying to manage my healing process* be my main responsibility in getting well?

Why pursuing deep relationship with God is so important is because Satan's final line of attack to keep us from getting well is to focus our attention on fighting to get well instead of on knowing God. As we see what the problem is, his lie is to encourage us to go after it in a misguided belief that resisting the sin in me *choices or even healing the* hurt of the heart *is something which we must personally manage. This is misdirection on a scale greater than that of the magician David Copperfield. We cannot fight our way to spiritual health. Never could. Never will. Paul records that the point when he realized his own weakness in being unable to change himself was when God's promised grace became effective in him (2 Corinthians 12:9).This is why he boasted in his weaknesses, so that he could see God do in him what he could not do for himself. Essentially, when we focus on the problem, we find that we have no attention left for the One who delivers and heals.*

3. On a scale of 1-10, how much guilt do you feel about your past life? On the same scale, how much anger do you have about your past life?

   • If guilt or anger is not what you feel, is there a different emotion you would use to describe your past life?
   • In what ways do these emotions affect your relationship with God?
   • Are you ready to get well? How do people get well?

4. In each of Paul's Ephesians pastoral prayers (1:17; 1:18-19; 3:14-19) he uses the word which we translate "know." He prays that they would know God better, know the hope, the riches and His power, and know the love of Christ. The word means more than knowledge out of a book. It means a knowledge that comes from experience. In what ways have you already experienced God, His gifts and His love in your life?

5. The first prayer Paul prays in Ephesians 1:17 is an intimacy prayer—that God would give to you the Spirit of wisdom and revelation so that you would know Him better." How do people generally come to know someone else better?

6. Review homework. What does Hebrews 4:14-16 tell you about why it is safe to be with God?

   - What did you learn about being with God without an agenda?
   - When were you in God's presence?
   - When were you aware that you were in God's presence?
   - What is rest in terms of a spiritual experience?
   - How is being before God without an agenda rest?
   - Why do you need to spend time before God resting?

7. Study Elijah's story in 1 Kings 19:1-18.

   - What happened to Elijah before he actually was ready to hear from God?
   - What do you think the wind, the earthquake and the fire in the story tell you about how we view God?

8. Read the following statement and answer the following question: Why do I personally need to be with God without an agenda?

Rest is being with God without an agenda. It means being ready to listen and hear what God has for you—mercy, grace, love, restoration. You may pray or read Scripture while you are with Him, but that rest is unstructured time with Him, allowing Him to guide you and reveal to you His desires for you. This is about building a personal relationship with God.

- Make time.
- Find a place apart from your daily activities and distractions.
- Go where you are physically comfortable while you are with God.
- It is good to tell God what you want from Him – peace, grace, mercy, etc.
- Read Scripture looking for God to speak.
- Review your day with God and acknowledge His presence during that day.
- Make being alone with God a regular part of your life. This is not a luxury. It is as essential as breathing and eating.

9. One important impact of the process is changing your belief about God the Father. In Matthew 5:8, Jesus tells us the pure at heart will see God. "Seeing God" is about seeing Him as He is, rather than the image we have projected on Him out of our fears and rebelliousness. One of the sources for our false image of God is our parents. What was your father or parents like? How might your view of your father or parents cloud your understanding of God?

10. It is time to rest in God's presence. During this time, you are invited to actively listen, to engage in the activities mentioned above. We will now go to different places to be alone with God and spend 20 minutes practicing rest. Enter into this time following this thinking:

First: *Approach* God within yourself without fear of rejection. This takes humility. You have no right to go into God's presence because you were good or bad. You have no right on your own. But He is inviting you. He wants you. And He has paid the price to remove all the barriers between you and Him. It's a humbling thing to go before God and say, "Here I am, I'm your child."

Second: *Believe* that He is with you and you are with Him. And that He is delivering what you need. You need mercy, compassion, comfort and affection. And you need grace—the power to do what God has for me to do.

Third: *Receive* tenderness and power even when you feel you deserve His judgment.

Assignment: Go rest in God's presence for 20 minutes.

11. Now that we are back, what did you experience with God, if anything? What did you learn about rest?

12. Dig a little deeper. What would you ask God about in dealing with the hurt in your heart the next time you rest in His presence?

Concluding Statement to be read out loud:

- *Understand this—you will not grow in your ability to rest by a quick session or two with God.*

- *Being with God without an agenda—but instead to hear and receive from Him—has a learning curve.*

- *You have to set aside time intentionally and you must get away from distractions.*

- *It may take months before you begin to sense you truly are ready to hear God when you are with Him. Why? Because we have busy minds. Instead of the ability to listen in quiet, we have cultivated a brain geared to short bursts of focus and multitasking.*

- *Do not give up this means of pursuing God. He is already there, and ready for you to know Him better.*

- *He has also given you His Spirit so this can be real in your life.*

- *Practice. Listen. Wait. Rest.*

- *In time, as you do this consistently, you will begin to have the kind of relationship with God you have always wanted, and more.*

At the end of this session: Pair up and pray with another person. Share something from your personal journey that you need prayer about. Then pray for the other person's need.

Homework Assignment: Next week we are going to look at a second practice that God offers you to bring transformation into your life—appropriation. In preparation for this session, read the following verses (Romans 5:10; Romans 6:4; Galatians 2:20; Colossians 3:1-4) and think on this question: How can I experience the reality of Christ living out his life in me?

Spend five minutes a day resting in God's presence.

SESSION 8: INTIMACY THROUGH APPROPRIATION

1. What have you learned from God so far? How has this new knowledge affected you emotionally? Spiritually?

2. Study the following chart.

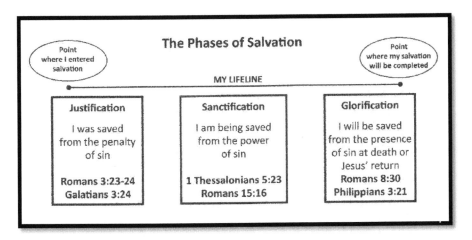

- Where are you in the salvation process now?
- What does that tell you about your faith journey?

3. Review homework. What do you understand about experiencing the reality of Christ living out his life in you? How do you apply this biblical truth to your faith journey?

4. Look up John 1:33, 14:25-26; Ephesians 1:13; Acts 1:8; 2:38; Romans 8:9-11; 2 Corinthians 3:17-19 and answer the following question: How is receiving the Spirit the game-changer in Jesus living his life out in us?

- How does having the Spirit explain the difference between being reformed in your character and being transformed into the likeness of Jesus?

5. In Hebrews 4:16, the writer makes a distinction between receiving mercy and obtaining grace from God.

    • How are these two gifts (mercy and grace) from God different?
    • How does grace relate to the presence of the Holy Spirit in you?
    • Look up Romans 8:29 again. What does grace do for you that you cannot do for yourself?
    • Look up 1 John 1:9 and see what God is doing when He gives mercy and when He applies grace.

6. Read the following statement and answer the question: Have you felt like there is anything you need from God in order to be saved from the power of sin—anything that you have not already been given?

Notice the progression here. Titus 2:11-14: "For the grace of God that brings salvation has appeared to all men. It teaches us to say "No" to ungodliness and worldly passions, and to live self-controlled, upright and godly lives in this present age, while we wait for the blessed hope—the glorious appearing of our great God and Savior, Jesus Christ (glorification), who gave himself for us to redeem us from all wickedness (justification) and to purify (sanctification) for himself a people that are his very own, eager to do what is good."

What is happening to us? We are being saved. What is the underlying power for that? The power for our salvation from the power of sin is the grace of God "that brings salvation and teaches us to say, "No." What you need to see is that you have everything you need from God to be made holy. You are not waiting for something. You don't have to pray for it. You don't have to get older in the Lord. You don't have to read the Bible more or anything like that. You don't have to wait for someone to come and lay hands on you. God has already given it to you. The issue is that we must appropriate or take hold of what God has already given us. We make this too hard. We start adding performance at this point and say we must stop doing this and start doing that. This is not about performance. If there's one thing I have to learn in the appropriation process it's that I have to rest. I have to stop trying to be good in my own strength. I can't beat what's wrong with me. I can't beat it by focusing on it either. Pay attention to that. You can't beat your symptoms, your addictions, your problems, by focusing on them. Sometimes counselors and Christian teachers get people so focused on what's wrong with them that they're worked up all the time. They're always beating themselves up. They're always worrying about the thing that they can't beat and they never rest. And resting has to do with focusing on intimacy with God. When I'm intimate with God the thing that is beating me will go away by His presence in my life.

- Why is this last question important?

7. The second prayer Paul prays in Ephesians 1:18-19 is an insight prayer. He is praying that his readers would know in an experiential way three things that they have been given by God as a result of putting their faith in Jesus. What are the hope, riches and power you have been given according to this passage?

  - Compare these verses with Ephesians 1:3 and 2 Peter 1:3-4. In what way has God equipped you to be saved from the power of sin? What do you get to do instead of having to sin?
  - When you are being tempted or are under spiritual attack, do you need to ask God to give you something more that He has already given you?
  - What do you understand 'appropriate' to mean for yourself?
  - Have you ever been denied something that was yours?
  - How do they make a difference in terms of your faith journey to being conformed to Jesus' likeness?

8. Look up Galatians 5:22-25. What is God giving us in exchange for the flesh life?

   • How does someone keep in step with the Spirit? Why is it important that you do so?

9. Read the following statement and answer this question: How does transformation differ from any self-improvement course you might try?

You are not just becoming a better person, but the Spirit is developing in you Christ's attributes as your primary character.

10. Dig a little deeper. What issue are you aware of in your faith journey right now for which you need to exercise appropriation?

11. Read the following statement and answer this question: What do you think will be your greatest challenge in developing awareness of your need for appropriation?

12. *Miles Stanford wrote years ago, "In order to appropriate something for our daily walk in Christ, there are two essentials: to see what is already ours in Christ and to be aware of our need for it." What I see holding so many people back from experiencing freedom from unfinished business is our failure to admit our need, rather than any lack in supply. It is our decision to avoid self-awareness that leaves us hopeless and open to the lies of the enemy that the sin in me is our only comfort.* Look up 2 Corinthians 2:11: Satan has a scheme to destroy you, one of which you may not be rationally aware. If that which is dying is drawing you towards death and that which is living is drawing you towards life, then how aware are you of what you are appropriating?

   • What do you need to do to change this if you have been unaware?

At the end of this session: Pair up and pray with another person. Share something from your personal journey that you need prayer about. Then pray for the other person's need.

Homework Assignment: Next week we are going to look at a third practice that God offers you to bring transformation into your life—meditation on the love of God. Take time this week to get apart from all of life's distractions. In the quiet, focus your mind on how much God loves you.

Spend five minutes a day resting in God's presence.

This week, when you sense the pull of *sin in me* choices, appropriate God's provision for you. Write down the results.

SESSION 9: INTIMACY THROUGH MEDITATION ON GOD'S LOVE

1. Review homework in light of the question: What have you learned from God so far? How has this new knowledge affected you emotionally? Spiritually?

2. Look up Colossians 1:6-14. According to these verses, what have you gained from being rescued by God? Also according to these verses, what can you expect to happen in your life as a result of God filling you with the knowledge of His will?

   - How often do you feel discouraged about where you are on your faith journey in relationship to what these verses affirm for you?
   - How secure do you sense that you are with God on your faith journey?
   - Why does it matter how secure you sense you are with God on your faith journey?

3. Look up Hebrews 8:7-13 and Luke 22:20. Throughout the Bible, God relates to people through covenant-making. In Jesus, he established a new covenant. According to verses 9-10, what is the critical difference between the old and new covenant?

   - What is God's stated outcome for this covenant according to verse 12? How does that affect you personally?

4. Read through Romans 8, which is Paul's practical application of the "save from the power of sin" effect of the new covenant on those who believe. Answer the following questions about the verses listed below:

Verses 1-4

- What does Paul mean in verse one when he says "there is now no condemnation for those in Christ Jesus?" How does that apply to you personally?
- According to verse 3, what was the law powerless to do for us? What does this suggest about God's reason for bringing about the new covenant through Jesus?
- In verse 4, what is God doing to us who have received the Spirit life?
- In what way does the Spirit life replace the flesh life?

Verses 15-16

- What were we afraid of when we were a slave to fear (see Ephesians 2:1-3)?

- How has the Spirit changed our relationship with God?

Verses 28-30

- What do the "all things" that God is working for good include in your life?
- Why is there not anything that you have done or will do in your life that is excluded from this activity of God?

Verses 31-39

- According to verses 33-34, when you are feeling like a failure in your faith journey or internally feeling condemned, where are these thoughts coming from?
- How does God respond to these accusations?
- Why is there nothing that ever can change how much God loves you?

- How secure are you in God's love?

5. Read the following statement and answer this question: What is the difference between feeling secure in God's love versus how secure you should be in God's love?

"God's love is more constant than human love can be. Human loving has its pure moments and parental love especially can sometimes express a likeness of God in its deep steadiness. But however solid it may be, human love is always prey to selfishness and distractions bred by attachment...It is not so with God's love. God goes on loving us regardless of who we are or what we do. This does not mean God is like a permissive human parent who makes excuses and ignores the consequences of a child's behavior. In God's constantly respectful love, consequences of our actions are very real, and they can be horrible, and we are responsible. We are even responsible for the compulsive behaviors of our addictions. The freedom God preserves in us has a double edge. On the one hand, it means God's love and empowerment are always with us. On the other, it means there is no authentic escape from the truth of our choices. But even when our choices are destructive and their consequences are hurtful, God's love remains unwavering." —Gerald May *in "Addiction and Grace"*

6. The third prayer Paul prays in Ephesians 3:14-19 is a transformational prayer. It has two parts, both pointing to God's power. The first part (verses 16-17) focuses on the ongoing empowering work of the Spirit so that Christ does not just live in your heart, but continually remodels it into his own place (based on the original wording). The second part (verses 17-19) speaks about how, being secure in God's love, you need to grasp as well as you can the full extent of God's love which will lead to continued and amazing transformation. The way you deepen your grasp on God's love is through the Done Discipline of meditating on the love of God. We are going to spend the next fifteen minutes meditating on God's love following these instructions:

- Meditation is possible when you step away from all of life's distractions. In the quiet, you *focus* your mind, not *empty* your mind. This is the critical difference between Christian mediation and eastern mystic meditation.

- During this time, ask God to give you a grasp on *one* of the following:
  1) How much God loves you.
  2) Why God chooses to love you.
  3) How much God loves those who wounded you.

- You may choose to look up one of these verses to give context to your meditation time:

  a. Philippians 1:6—He who began a good work in you will complete it
  b. 1 John 7-9—God is love
  c. 1John 3:1—we will be called the children of God
  d. Psalm 34:4—God delivered me from all fears
  e. Romans 8:37-39—nothing can separate you from God's love

  Assignment: Go meditate for 15 minutes.

7. What did you learn during this time of meditation?

8. The more you practice this Done Discipline, the greater you will sense that you are safe with God and your trust in Him will grow.

   - How do you think that this deepening intimacy with God will help you in the face of the accusations, temptations and lies of the enemy?

   - How do you think that this deepening intimacy with God will help you really forgive the people who wounded you?

9. Read Matthew 6:12, 14; Mark 11:24-26. Forgiveness is at the heart of unbroken intimacy with God. For what person(s) do you need to trust God to give you true forgiveness so you can continue to deepen your intimacy with Him?

    *   What help do you need from others to move forward in forgiveness?
    *   Can we pray for you right now that you will appropriate the grace and peace of God to be able to forgive the person(s) who wounded you?

At the end of this session: Pair up and pray with another person. Share something from your personal journey that you need prayer about. Then pray for the other person's need.

Homework Assignment: Next week we are preparing ourselves for going on in our faith journey applying the truths we have learned through this study. To be ready for this last lesson, read through Matthew 5:3-10, which are the eight Beatitudes that Jesus taught at the beginning of what we call the Sermon on the Mount. Be ready to discuss the Beatitude that is most challenging for you.

Spend five minutes a day resting in God's presence.

This week, when you sense the pull of sin in me choices, appropriate God's provision for you. Write down the results.

Spend ten minutes this week meditating on God's love.

SESSION 10: GOING ON WITH YOUR FAITH JOURNEY

1. Look up 1 Corinthians 2:10-16 and answer the following question: Why has God given us His Spirit?

   - How does this truth connect to keeping in step with the Spirit (Galatians 5:25)?

   - How far have I come in learning to trust the Holy Spirit's work in me?

   - It takes time to deepen your intimacy with God to the point where you will trust Him enough to allow Him to deal with unfinished business in your life. So how will you deal with discouragement when it comes and change is slow, when temptation still seems to own you and your thoughts, during these early stages of pursuing God?

2. Read the following story and answer the following question: Why have I used other people or activities to make myself feel better?

*Hannah Whitall Smith, author of "The Christian's Secret to a Happy Life," tells that when she was a young wife and mother, she came to a place where she could not take the accumulated hurts and crises of her life. She was crying a lot and was very depressed. Finally, she thought that she would go and share her burdens with a godly older woman she knew. She made an appointment and, on that day, poured out her soul to the woman. Her friend listened quietly and after a long pause, said, "Well, after all, there **is** God." Thinking that the woman had not understood, Hannah again went through a full listing of all that was wrong in her world. Again, the woman said thoughtfully, "After all, there **is** God." Hannah asked if this was all. Being told it was all, she became angry and went home in a huff. She did not see what good this advice could possibly be—further, she did not really understand what the advice was. But she reflected on the character of this lady, and* *began to pray about the advice. And she discovered for herself that the statement was the answer—that all other wisdom and advice she had thought to try had been inadequate. She came to see that the answers to her dilemmas were not going to be found in external change and methods, but in relationship with God.*

- How will intimacy with God bring real healing in me?
- Reflecting back to the story about the man who had been sick for 38 years Jesus encountered beside the pool of Bethesda, picking up the mat was Jesus' invitation to get well. Picking up the mat is doing what God is telling you to do at this moment. What mat is God telling you to pick up?

3. Review homework. Which Beatitude is most challenging for you?

4. The order of the Beatitudes in Matthew 5:3-10 suggests progressive transformation, starting with acknowledging that you have nothing in you that will make you into the person God created you to be. This is not just a one-time occurrence, but is a recurring cycle in your transformational process. You will need to continually come again to the end of believing the lie that the *hurt of the heart* of which you are aware at this moment can be dealt with by anything other than God Himself. You are then ready to humbly allow Him to free you from the power of *sin in me* choices by focusing on intimacy with Him. Walk through the eight Beatitudes together and discuss their implications for your faith journey.

a) **Poor In Spirit:** *Being Humbled by My Spiritual Poverty,* which is the point I recognize that I have neither the ability within me nor the power to remake myself into the person I was created to be.

b) **Mourn:** *Grieving Properly* over the wounds I have received from living in a fallen world, while recognizing that I have, in turn, wounded others as well.

c) **Meek:** *Submitting Totally* to the reign of God over me so that I can live in this world in the manner I was intended to live by God.

d) **Hunger And Thirst:** *Refocusing Desires* toward wanting what God wants, allowing myself to be restored to the likeness of His Son.

e) **Merciful:** *Growing Compassion* for those who are wounded, including those who wounded me.

f) **Pure In Heart:** *Seeing God Clearly* to the point that I stop projecting false images on Him drawn from my experiences with human figures of authority, including my parents, and stop believing lies about Him due to these false images.

g) **Peacemakers:** *Conforming to Jesus* who is our peace, and who is the one who offers peace and restoration to all who have rebelled and rejected God.

h) **Persecuted:** *Anticipating Opposition* from friends, family and even religious people as I progressively am becoming the person I was created to be.

- Why do you think you need to recognize that your faith journey will be a progressive one?
- Look up Revelation 12:10. If you experience failure along this faith journey, who will be the one who will accuse you and seek to use your failure against you?
- According to Romans 8:31-34, what will be God's attitude and action towards you?

- Do you think there will come a time when Satan's lies can no longer draw you back into destructive behavior and distrust of God? Why or why not?

5. Look up 2 Samuel 11:1-14. Who is King David and what was he known for (Acts 13:22)?

  - How successful had God made David in his life up to this point?
  - Since it was the time of year when "kings went off to war," what do you think was happening when David sent his army but did not go with them?
  - What do the actions he takes after staying home suggest about his heart?
  - What does his decision about what to do with Uriah tell you about the ongoing dangers of secret keeping?

6. Look up 2 Chronicles 16:7-12. Who is King Asa and what was he known for (2 Chronicles 15:16-19)?

  - Why was Asa mad at God?
  - Why do you think he ended up suffering from physical pain during the last years of his life?
  - What does his decision about his relationship to God tell you about the danger of becoming attached to internal lies about God?

7. Read the following statement and answer the following question: What do you think would make you most vulnerable to Satan's lies?

We don't really know what the growth process will look like. Sometimes people say, "Oh I'm committed to Christ no matter what. Except that we thought that everything was going to go well. We might think that commitment means we're not going to have problems. And then we have problems and then we're angry or upset because it's not fair. We're committed, so we think the path should be smooth! There shouldn't be any friction.

I don't know what I might face in the future. There could be some really hard things ahead of me. In making a commitment to God I say I'm going to trust Him no matter what happens to me. But I don't know what will happen to me. When I get to those difficult situations I'd like to believe that I will still trust God. I could go backwards. At that moment I could choose to say, "God I don't care what you've done for me in the past, this thing that is happening to me right now is just too much. I'm going to control this one for myself because it looks like, "You've deserted me," or "You're just not paying attention to what's going on here." Or I might say, "At this moment what has happened to me is so horrible that I hate you, God."

People do that. And at that moment they make horrible decisions in their lives. You might look at them and say, "Why would they ever choose to do something so destructive? Look what God has already done in their lives. Look at what God has done in my life. Why would I ever choose to get into an affair, or hurt my children, or cuss somebody out, or eat myself into the hospital, or shoplift, or something else equally degrading and sinful. I don't know why I'd choose to do that but I don't know what I'm going to face either.

Total commitment is a daily choice. What we need to grasp is that there must be a point where we choose to trust the Father—no matter what.

- Why, then, should you personally have mercy on others around you, even those who you consider bad people? What would mercy look like?

8. Read the following statement and discuss what it means for you to go on, intentionally building a relationship with God.

We must be intentional about commitment. I do what I intend to do. I am saying in this commitment that I will not be passive in the growing and healing process, waiting for God to hit me over the head and push me out of my recliner. Instead, I will yield myself to Jesus, and actively pursue a relationship with Him, who is according to John 1:14, full of grace (God's empowerment) and truth (what I was created to be). God's purpose is to conform me into the likeness of His Son, so when we talk about Jesus being full of grace and truth we are looking at what I am created to be—like Jesus—full of grace and truth.

I learned how deeply satisfying this is a long time after I submitted myself to God at the start of my journey. I had always been critical of my wife since our marriage. I arrogantly found that she did not measure up to my standards of doing things—how she kept house, how she raised the children, etc. I foolishly sought to fix her through pointing out her faults, thinking that in time she would get better. I had no idea how badly I was wounding her and destroying our marriage.

One day, soon after I entered into the healing process with God, He showed me I was to stop criticizing my wife. I was staggered, but because now I wanted what God wanted, I submitted willingly, asking that He do this in me by His grace. A year later, conditions had so changed in our marriage that my wife, who journaled her thoughts, wrote in her notebook that day all the reasons she loved me as her husband. The first statement she wrote was, "I love my husband because he doesn't criticize me." I first saw this list seventeen years later, on a day when my wife was cleaning out her storage chest. When she handed me the list, I was dumbstruck at the confirmation of God's changing our marriage by changing me years before. Through that one act of obedience love was rekindled in my wife.

9. How do you plan to go on from here? Discuss the following
    practical steps:

- How will I seek to make my own what I learned during these sessions?
- Where do I plan to incorporate the "Done" Disciplines regularly into my faith journey so that I can grow in my intimacy with God? Who will I ask to help hold me accountable in the initial stages of making these a regular part of my life?
- What aspects of Jesus' life and character should I study to gain insight into what I am to become?
- According to 2 Peter 1:5-9, what else should I seek to see developed in my life to be productive in my faith? How would I go about developing them?
- Who is someone who needs to hear this—that I can regularly share with what I am learning? When will I start the process?

10. A last point. Look up 1 Peter 5:5b-11.

- What is it that we need most of all to access God's grace?
- Why do we need to be self-controlled and pay attention to the activity of the enemy?
- Who is on your side in all this?

At the end of this session: Pair up and pray with another person. Share something from your personal journey that you need prayer about. Then pray for the other person's need.

Ongoing Assignment: Continue to practice the "Done" Disciplines in pursuit of intimacy with God and the freedom Jesus promised through the gospel ("It is for freedom that Christ has set us free." Galatians 5:1). Confess your sins to others in community and be healed.

APPENDIX A: COLOSSIANS 1-3

Chapter 1

V 5: I have hope stored up for me in Heaven in Christ Jesus.

V 11: I am strengthened with all power according to His glorious might in Christ Jesus.

V 12: I am qualified to share in the inheritance of the kingdom in Christ Jesus.

V 13: I have been rescued & delivered in Jesus.

V 14: I am redeemed and forgiven in Christ Jesus.

V 16: I am His creation.

V 17: I am held together by Christ Jesus.

V 18: I am a part of the body of Jesus Christ.

V 19: I have the fullness of God in Jesus.

V 20: I am reconciled to God in Jesus.

V 22-23: I am reconciled, holy, free from blemish & accusation if I stand firm in His performance (not mine).

V 26: I have the mystery revealed in Christ Jesus.

V 27: I have Christ in me, the hope of glory.

V 29: I have the energy of Christ with which to struggle.

Chapter 2

V 3: I am in Christ, where all the treasures of wisdom and knowledge are hidden.

V 6: I have received Christ Jesus as Lord.

V 7: As I live in Him, I am rooted, built up and established in faith in Christ Jesus.

V 9: I am Christ, and in Christ, all the fullness of Deity dwells.

V 10: I have fullness in Jesus.

V 11: My sinful nature has been cut off of me in Christ Jesus.

V 12: I have been buried with Him in baptism and raised with Him through faith.

V 13: I am dead in my trespasses, made alive, and forgiven in Christ Jesus.

V 14: I am no longer ruled by the old regulations.

V 15: In Christ, powers and authorities against my life have been disarmed by the cross.

V 17: I have reality in Christ Jesus.

V 20: I am dead to the world's principles in Jesus.

Chapter 3

V 1: I am raised with Christ, seated at the right hand of God.

V 3: I died to this world, and am alive, but hidden in Christ.

V 4: I have been promised that I will appear with Him in glory.

V 9: I have put off the old self in Christ.

V 10: In Jesus, I am a new man and renewed in knowledge.

V 12: I am chosen, holy, dearly loved in Christ Jesus.

V 13: I am forgiven in Christ Jesus.

V 15: I am a member of one body in Jesus Christ.

V 24: I am an heir of the reward of inheritance through Christ Jesus.

Appendix B: Ephesians 1-3

Chapter 1

V 3: I am blessed with every spiritual blessing in Christ Jesus.

V 4: I am chosen in Christ Jesus.

V 5: I am adopted in Christ Jesus, in accordance with His pleasure.

V 6: I have grace freely given to me in Christ Jesus.

V 7: I am redeemed in Christ Jesus (repurchased). I am forgiven in Christ Jesus (to be cleansed, set free).

V 8: I am lavished upon by God's riches and grace, with all wisdom and understanding.

V 10: I am being brought together under one head in Christ.

V 11: I am chosen in Christ Jesus. I am predestined in Christ Jesus, I have been put into a situation where God is going to get His way.

V 12: I am predestined to be the praise of His glory.

V 13: I am included in Christ Jesus. I am sealed in Christ Jesus.

V 14: I am God's possession.

V 17: I have access to the spirit of wisdom and revelation. I have access to especially knowing Jesus Christ, the glorious Father and the Holy Spirit.

V 18: I have been called to a hope. I have been called to a glorious inheritance.

V 19: I can know His great power.

V 22: I am under His feet (He dominates me).

V 23: I am a part of His body, which is the fullness of Him who fills everything in every way.

Chapter 2

V 4: I am loved by God who is rich in mercy.

V 5: I am made alive with Christ. I am saved in Christ Jesus.

V 6: I am raised up with Christ. I am seated in the heavenly realm with Him in Christ Jesus.

V 7: I am an object of the incomparable riches of His grace. I have God's kindness in Christ Jesus.

V 8: I am saved by grace in Christ Jesus as a gift from God.

V 10: I am God's workmanship I Christ Jesus. I am created to do good works in Christ Jesus.

V 13: I am brought near to God in Christ Jesus.

V 14: I am at peace in Christ Jesus.

V 15: I am a part of one new man in Christ Jesus.

V 16: I am reconciled to God in Christ Jesus.

V 18: I have access to the Father by one Spirit.

V 19: I am a citizen of God's household in Christ Jesus. I am a member of God's household in Christ Jesus.

V 20: I am built on a foundation with Christ Jesus as the chief cornerstone.

V 21: I am a holy temple in Christ Jesus.

V 22: Corporately, I am becoming a dwelling for God's Spirit in Christ Jesus.

Chapter 3

V 6: I am heir to all of Israel's promises. I am a member of one body in Christ Jesus. I am a sharer in the promise in Christ Jesus.

V 8: I have access to the unsearchable riches in Christ Jesus.

V 9: The mystery once hidden in God can be made plain to me in Christ Jesus.

V 10: It is His intention to make known the manifold wisdom of God through me.

V 11: He has already accomplished His intention.

V 12: I am free to approach God in Christ Jesus. I am confident to approach God in Christ Jesus.

V 15: My name comes from God.

V 16: I am strengthened through His Spirit in my inner being (if I so choose)

V 17: By choice I am the dwelling place of Christ.

V 19: I can know the love of Christ that surpasses knowledge (if I so choose). I can be filled to the measure of all the fullness of God (if I so choose).

V 20: His power is at work within me.

Church
Equippers

For additional tools, please visit:

www.ChurchEquippers.com

Made in the USA
San Bernardino, CA
01 May 2017